Little Learning Labs

ART
FOR KIDS

**26 Adventures
in Drawing, Painting,
Mixed Media
and More**

QUARRY

SUSAN SCHWAKE

Brimming with creative inspiration, how-to projects, and useful
information to enrich your everyday life, Quarto Knows is a favorite
destination for those pursuing their interests and passions. Visit our
site and dig deeper with our books into your area of interest:
Quarto Creates, Quarto Cooks, Quarto Homes, Quarto Lives,
Quarto Drives, Quarto Explores, Quarto Gifts, or Quarto Kids.

10 9 8 7 6 5 4 3 2 1

ISBN: 978-1-63159-566-0

Digital edition published in 2018
The content in this book originally appeared in the book *Art Lab
for Kids* (Quarry Books, 2012).

Design: John Hall Design Group, www.johnhalldesign.com
Cover Image: Rainer Schwake
Page Layout: tabula rasa graphic design

Printed in China

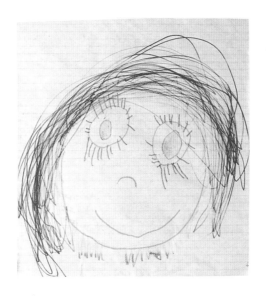

This book is dedicated with love to my mother,
who always nurtured the artist in me.

Contents

Introduction

THIS BOOK IS A SMATTERING OF LESSONS I have used over the past twenty years of teaching. They started on the kitchen table with my daughter, Grace, when she was three. Two years and a second baby (Chloe) later, I was convinced that I had to take the art lessons out of the home and share them with others. I opened my little art school in a rented space at a local church. A year passed, and the classes expanded. I moved into a larger studio, then a second location. Finally, it grew up fully into the gallery/studio/school it is today.

Almost every art lesson I taught along the way shared stories about or pictures from contemporary artists. It has been my belief that, through viewing the art of a wide variety of artists, students can identify with a particular movement or singular artist's work. This can reassure young artists of their own work, their own vision.

In our gallery, I curate ten exhibits a year with groups of contemporary artists. The students view the work on a weekly basis, in their classes. Along with the exhibits, books, slides, Internet sites, and posters introduce my students to a broad range of art. However, nothing can replace seeing the actual artwork. I highly recommend visiting a local gallery or museum to see the paintings, drawings, prints, and other artwork in person. It can change your life!

How to Use This Book

THIS BOOK IS FOR ANYONE interested in making art with others—or alone. Each Lab is a separate lesson; some are traditionally based; others are not. The units are grouped by medium, and there is some crossover in materials from one Unit to another. The Labs are set up loosely to build skills upon the previous ones; however, you may begin anywhere. Each Lab is a stand-alone project.

In this Unit, I outline what you will need to set up a studio. The list is comprehensive, but you do not need much to get started. I also provide basic steps for using the materials that appear in many of the Labs.

Some Important Ideas about Making Art with Others

- Each person's work should be wholly his or her own. Don't work on someone else's art. Use thoughtful language when working with others. For example, "Tell me about your painting" works better than "What is that?"
- Always use the best materials that you can lay your hands on for each art-making session. Paper weight makes a big difference in the outcome of a watercolor painting, but you can use recycled flat cardboard with gesso as a primer for acrylic painting.
- Don't worry about wrecking a new paper or canvas. These items can be reused—torn up for collage, primed over with gesso, or printed over.
- Promote fearlessness.
- Embrace individual style. Respect each other's differences.

These Labs are jumping-off points. Explore them with the Go Further suggestions. Try out your own ideas. Have fun! The most important lessons in art are the ones that you discover about yourself in the process. Be brave, experiment, and fear no art!

The Master List

A creative place for making art is best fashioned in a comfortable environment, a place free from worry about making a mess. Making art can be stressful for some people—many think it means making a mess or creating havoc. Worry no more! As with so many things in life, preparation is the key to success, and a deeper understanding of a situation is a powerful tool.

The following is a list of items, from simple furnishings to basic materials, to help you build your artmaking space. Collecting these supplies over time is the easiest and most cost-effective way to gather them; however, you might already have many of these items. Keep them in labeled boxes on shelves for easy storage.

1. Natural light or good overhead lighting. Task lighting, such as a clip-on lamp on a desk or table, is useful in smaller group situations.
2. A sturdy table with chairs set at the appropriate height for the student. The height of the table should be approximately at the student's waist, and, when seated, the student's feet should be on the floor.
3. A plastic table covering to protect the surface. Secure it with strong tape to keep it from slipping around.
4. A nearby water source. The best situation is a sink in the room, but buckets of water can work well, with some empty buckets available for dumping dirty water. A plastic tarp or tablecloth under the buckets helps protect the floor.
5. Small plastic containers—round and rectangular, small and large—for holding water.
6. Newspapers, good for just about everything in the mess-control business.
7. Boxes, totes, or shelves for holding supplies. Label them to make finding things easier.
8. Plexiglas or Perspex sheets, about 8" x 10" (20 x 25 cm) in size, one for each student, to use as a palette for painting, printmaking, and drawing. They last forever and are easy to clean.
9. Wax paper and aluminum foil.

10. Fiberboard or Masonite for holding paper securely for drawing or painting.
11. Rolls of clear tape, masking tape, and duct tape.
12. Smocks for protecting the artist. Large men's shirts work well for this, as do old T-shirts.
13. Paper of all sorts: 24-lb. copy paper, 80-lb. sketching paper, 90- or 140-lb. watercolor paper, heavy cardstock, and a collection of fancy colored papers of your choice.
14. Markers of all colors and thicknesses, as well as black permanent markers, crayons, oil pastels, soft pastels, pencils in a variety of hardness, vine charcoal, colored pencils, kneaded erasers, white plastic erasers, and pencil sharpeners.
15. Watercolor pan paints, acrylic paints (both liquid and heavy bodied), tempera paint, gouache, and India ink.
16. Water-based printmaking ink in black and colors.
17. Brayers for printmaking and mixed-media work.
18. Soft-haired brushes for watercolor and ink and nylon or bristle brushes for acrylic, in a variety of sizes and shapes.
19. Recycled items, including magazines, greeting cards, candy wrappers, old letters, graph paper, colored wrapping paper, maps, old photographs, discarded artwork, discarded books, stickers, stamp pads, balls of string and yarn, embroidery floss, embroidery hoops, small fabric scraps, buttons, textile trims, carded wool, old mats and frames, and poly-foam filling.
20. Found objects for printing or texturing paper; these can include corks, wooden blocks, small sponges, metal washers, corrugated cardboard, lace, craft sticks, pencils with erasers, cookie cutters, straws, plastic toys, tiny cars, cardboard tubes, assorted hardware items, Styrofoam, buttons, and any other items with an interesting shape. Plastic texture plates are available from art suppliers both online and in stores.

Making a Good Still-Life Composition

- Choose everyday items that are familiar to you. Don't overlook the simple.
- Vary the height of your objects; for example, try tall bottles with short bowls.
- Vary your textures; include shiny, matte, bumpy, and irregular surfaces.

21. Adhesives, such as white glue, clear glue, tacky glue, glue sticks, E6000 extra-strong glue, and wood glue, as well as a hot glue gun with glue melt sticks.

22. Canvas boards, canvas paper, stretched canvas, found wood, smooth birch plywood, and fiberboard or Masonite. All should be primed for painting with an acrylic gesso.

23. Kitchen supplies, such as liquid soap, plastic bowls, wooden spoons, sponges, scrub brushes, drinking straws, old cookie sheets, paper towels, rags, clean recycled foam trays from the grocery store, butcher paper, and plastic cutlery.

24. Office supplies, including rulers, stapler, paper clips, bulldog clips, push pins, rubber stamps, and rubber bands.

25. Hardware supplies: hammer, screwdriver, nails, screws, tape measure, metal washers, sandpaper of varying grit, paint-can openers, and foam brushes.

26. A cardboard portfolio to keep work together, or an old magazine rack, a deep drawer or shelf.

27. A display area for finished work; this can be a cork board, a string with clips, or wall space.

Setting Up an Area for Drawing

Most drawing lessons require little setup and cleanup, and, with the exception of India ink, there is little to spill. Keep India ink in small refillable bottles or shallow containers, and always work on newspaper to protect surfaces from the ink.

When using soft pastels or charcoal, have a damp paper towel nearby to keep your fingers clean.

Make drawing boards to use as a drawing surface (if you are drawing outside or without a table) from pieces of Masonite or thick foamcore. Masking tape or bulldog clips keep paper securely affixed.

Spray fixatives for charcoal and soft pastel should be used only by an adult and applied only outside. To prevent spatters, hold the can at arm's length, and spray with a sweeping motion across the paper.

Setting Up an Area for Painting

Setting up your workspace makes creating much simpler; when everything is in order, it's easier to focus on painting.

Protect the table with butcher paper, a plastic tablecloth, or newspaper and the floor (if necessary) with a reusable tarp or tablecloth.

Place a folded sheet of newspaper on the right side of your paper if you are right-handed and on the left if you are left-handed. This is where you put your water container, brushes, and Plexiglas paint palette. An extra piece of paper folded in half again is good for wiping off water or excess paint. Set it up this way and you will avoid most accidents.

For acrylic paints, dispense coin-size amounts, add retarder to slow down the drying time, and mix paints with palette knives for easy cleanup. For gouache, a shallow-welled palette for holding small amounts of water and paint works well. Slip a piece of white scrap paper under the edge of your palette for testing colors. When finished with an acrylic painting, you can protect the work by brushing an acrylic varnish over it evenly, or you can spray the work outdoors with a clear-coat finish under adult supervision.

Setting Up an Area for Printmaking

Start your printmaking experience by grabbing a stack of newspaper. Open up five sheets to cover your work area. Layering it is best, up to ten sheets, so you can pull away the inky ones and always have a fresh one underneath as you go. Have a shallow rectangular container of water handy to wash the brayers off when changing colors during the process. Have your clean printing paper in a stack nearby but not on your work surface. Number them in pencil in edition form, as instructed below, and sign them. Have a square of damp paper towel near your water container to wipe off your fingers if they get too inky.

Use the Plexiglas palette (or polystyrene plate or tray) for your ink station and a second piece for monotypes. When inking, roll the ink away from you slowly, in line with the width of your brayer and the length of your Plexiglas, or less. Pull the brayer back toward you and continue to roll until the ink is smooth. You can also use foam trays for the ink. Now you are ready to print!

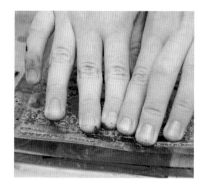

Paper and Mixed Media

Paper, from junk mail to beautiful handmade papers, can be collected from many sources. For mixed media, consider using old letters, stamps, wrappers, greeting cards, ticket stubs, old books, dictionaries, wallpaper sample books, graph paper, ledger paper, gift wrapping, and cardboard from cereal boxes. Keep a box for your papers and a small envelope for tiny pieces too beautiful to throw away.

GLUING, TEARING, AND CUTTING PAPER

To keep your artwork from getting sticky, place a piece of scrap paper under your project when gluing paper pieces onto your artwork.

Tearing paper produces a different look from cutting paper. Torn paper gives an organic look, with soft edges; cut paper is sharp and hard-edged.

Paper has a grain just like the wood it's made from. Tearing with the grain is easiest to control. Try this with newspaper to experiment! Tearing across the grain is more difficult. With a colored or printed paper, pulling the paper from the top to the bottom with your right hand leaves the left side of the paper with a white border. Sometimes that white edge or border is perfect for a special outlined look. Keep your fingers pinched close together for the most controlled tearing.

When tearing thick, handmade paper, first draw a line with a wet brush along the tear line, then pull the paper apart.

Cutting paper always gives a crisp edge. If your paper is large, you might want to cut it down before making your detail cuts. Trying to cut a small piece out of the middle of a large piece of paper is challenging. Cut in, to get to it, and then remove the excess around it.

Drawing

DRAWING IS A FOUNDATION SKILL FOR ALL ART. It can excite or intimidate students, depending on where they are on their artistic journey. This Unit will allow students to explore drawing in ways beyond the pencil and paper. Each Lab encourages fearless markmaking and thoughtful line and volume work. Some Labs incorporate a brush and ink or bright watercolors; others use more traditional media. When practicing drawing, many people find the eraser to be their best friend and their worst enemy. For many years, I didn't have erasers readily available for my students, because some spent more time erasing lines than drawing them. I found that, through the use of different media, many students found success, where the pencil and eraser had failed them before. It has been my desire to encourage every student through unconventional methods, endless exploration, and allowing chance to be a viable element in their drawing. Remember, this should be fun! Keep the fun part in mind when embarking on any of these Labs—experience is the focus—not perfection.

UNIT

1

Contour Drawings

- drawing paper
- permanent black marker, thin or thick point
- soft pencil
- charcoal
- still life made up of simple objects, such as fruit, bottles, bowls, vases, and boxes

Think First: Contour drawing is one way to begin any two-dimensional artwork. Arrange your objects so some of them overlap and some have spaces between them. Take a few moments to look at the edges of each of the objects you have placed in your composition. Trace your finger around them in the air to get a feel for their edges. Starting an artwork with a good contour drawing can be very helpful!

Go Further

- Perform this exercise in your sketchbook each day for a month, using different objects
- Make a "blind contour" drawing by looking at the objects only, not the paper, while you are drawing. This is a great way to improve your ability to "see" the object and train your hand with your eye.

Let's Go!

Fig. 1: Follow the edges with your eye to draw them.

1. After studying the edges of the objects, begin drawing them with the permanent marker, from one side of the composition to the other. Some people like to work from the background to the front. Try both ways to find your favorite (fig. 1).

2. Remember to eliminate all of the extras—just outline the objects.

Fig. 2: Leave out details and draw just the outline.

3. Continue to draw all of the objects until they are all sketched in (fig. 2).

4. Draw the same still life with the soft pencil and then with the charcoal (fig. 3).

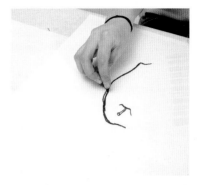

Fig. 3: Try the same drawing with charcoal.

5. Enjoy the process of getting to know your composition through contour drawing with three different materials. You can finish off your artwork with color if you desire.

Meet the Artist:
Rose Sielian Theriault

Rose Theriault, an artist from New Hampshire, has taught high school art for more than thirty years. She works in a variety of media and loves still life drawing and etching. *Pears Squared* is an etching showing the essence of contour drawing. Rose uses this technique often in her bold and beautiful work.

Pears Squared by Rose Sielian Theriault

Large-Scale Ink Drawings

Materials

- large piece of drawing or watercolor paper
- black ink
- medium-size watercolor brush
- assorted soft pastels or pan watercolor
- container of water
- paper towels
- newspaper
- still life composed of bottles and fruit sitting on a cloth or large piece of paper

Think First: Arrange the still life in front of your working area. You want to be able to see all of it but still have space for your drawing paper. Make sure the objects are not too far apart from one another—try a few different arrangements until you are happy with it. Have a seat in front of your paper and still life and decide what you would like to include in your artwork. Remember, the paper is large and you will be making the objects larger than life-size, so think about their placement.

Choose what to draw after setting up your still life.

Let's Go!

Fig. 1: Begin with the objects in the back first, then work your way to the front.

1. After thinking about what parts of the still life you are going to draw, begin with the objects farthest away from you (fig. 1).

2. Using the ink and the brush, without drawing first with a pencil, might seem scary to begin with, but be brave and make your marks boldly and large!

Meet the Artist: Ernst Kirchner

Ernst Kirchner has a strong distinctive style and often uses ink in his drawings and paintings. He helped found the Brücke artists association in 1905. He enjoyed capturing city street scenes with groups of people. His work *Cocotte with Dog* inspired this Lab. Read more about Ernst Kirchner at www.bruecke-museum .de/englkirchner.htm.

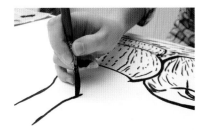

Fig. 2: Be brave!

Fig. 3: Shadows are part of the drawing too; add them with ink or color.

3. Working from the back to the front, draw the still life with the paintbrush, adding all the details that you want to have in black ink. Watch for overlapping objects, and remember to pick up your brush when you come to an overlapping line. Work from one side to the other to avoid smearing your work with your arm (fig. 2).

Fig. 4: Watercolor is a good choice for adding color if you have used a heavier paper.

4. Shadows can be added with ink or with pastel or watercolor (fig. 3).

5. After the work is dry, add soft pastel for color and for shadows, or use some watercolor if you have used watercolor paper.

6. After you add color, you can go back over your black lines with ink to make them crisp (fig. 4).

Go Further

• Try drawing a portrait of yourself with your family's pet.

• Use only ink, and, instead of color, use shapes or lines to create interest in the shadows, details, and background.

Scribble Drawings

- drawing paper
- pencil
- colored pencils
- optional: watercolors
- scissors
- glue stick for paper
- background papers you have made or bought
- paper towels and newspapers (if using watercolors)

Think First: This lesson draws on your ability to let go and scribble. It also engages the part of you that enjoys lying on your back in the grass, looking up at the clouds, and seeing things in the shapes the clouds make. So, relax! Get loose! Imagine things!

Go Further

- Collect smaller cut-out scribbles to create a large collage artwork.
- Instead of colored pencils, try watercolors for details, if you use heavy paper.

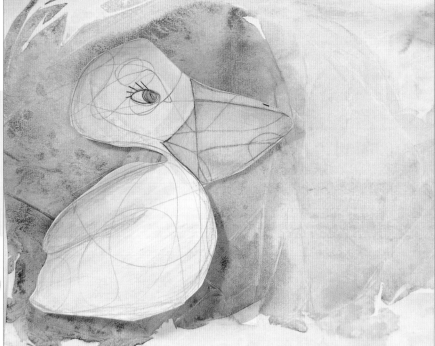

Finished scribble drawing which has been cut out and glued onto a background

Let's Go!

Fig. 1: *Keep your drawing loose and loopy.*

Fig. 2: *Outline your objects first with pencil.*

1. Using a pencil, start scribbling in a circular motion, one long line all over your paper (fig. 1).

2. Keep your pencil in contact with the paper at all times, making the scribble in one long motion. Cross often over the lines you have made!

3. Stop when you see there are enough lines on your paper. Do this on at least two pieces of paper.

4. Examine the scribble by holding it up in front of you and turning the paper in all directions. Find objects in the scribble. Outline them with your pencil so they are more apparent (fig. 2). You might not find something in your scribble on your own. If this happens, have a friend take a look at your scribble. She will find something!

5. Using colored pencils, add details and color to the objects you have found (fig. 3).

Fig. 3: *With colored pencil, add details.*

Fig. 4: *Cut out your drawings.*

6. Cut out the objects or add a background, if you prefer (fig. 4).

7. If you cut them out, find a background paper where your scribble drawings could live and glue them onto that paper with a glue stick.

Meet the Artist: Anne O. Smith

Anne O. Smith is an artist and retired high school art teacher. Her whimsical work includes lots of scribble drawings. A big scribble that she cut out and then redrew became the art piece *Bird Walk*.

Bird Walk by Anne O. Smith

Soft Pastel Drawings

Materials

- drawing or pastel paper
- soft pastels
- bouquet of flowers
  (real flowers are great,
  but silk ones will work, too)
- a vase
- fixative

Deciding on a composition

Think First: Set up your still life. Study the flowers. The petals and leaves of each flower have different shapes. Take some time to see each petal and trace it with your finger, first on the flower and then in the air. Is it pointed or rounded? Do the petals have more than one color? Where are they lightest and where are they darkest? Decide if you want to zoom in on a few blooms to fill your page or if you want to draw the entire bouquet. Choosing your composition (what your drawing is going to include and where the objects sit on the paper) now is a good thing.

Let's Go!

1. Look at your paper and decide which way it should be oriented: horizontally or vertically. Using the pastels, start drawing the vase. If you are zoomed in very close, begin with the largest bloom.

2. Remember that pastels smudge easily, so keep your hand above the paper as you draw. Press lightly—the color flows easily from soft pastels.

3. Continue working out to the edges of your composition with the pastels.

4. Try layering colors, one on top of the other, to get the full range of colors in the petals (fig. 1).

5. Try smudging two colors with your finger to blend them into a new color.

6. Make short marks and long marks for a nice variation in texture (fig. 2).

7. Finish the drawing with a fixative to reduce smudging, as described on page 11.

Fig. 1: *Layer pastel colors.*

Fig. 2: *Create texture with different kinds of lines.*

Meet the Artist: Mitchell Rosenzweig

Mitchell Rosenzweig is an accomplished artist living in the Greater New York City area. His work ranges from pastels to paintings—often very large—and sculptures. *Wild Sky over Mountains* is one of his beautiful pastel paintings. Find out more about Mitchell's work at mitchellrosenzweig.com.

Wild Sky over Mountains by Mitchell Rosenzweig

Go Further

- Pastels are also a fun medium to use to make portraits and landscapes.

- Try an abstract pastel painting. Start with a shape and repeat the shape, adding lines in between, or a try using pastels for a scribble drawing as in Lab 3!

Materials

- drawing-weight paper
- oil pastels
- still life objects (think favorite toy: plush, plastic, wooden, doll)
- small box or container to raise up the objects
- cloth to cover the box, if desired

Think First: Oil pastels are colorful and creamy in texture. If you like the way an oil painting looks, you will love creating your own masterpiece with oil pastels!

Set up a still life with boxes and some simple (shaped) objects. Make your still life personal by adding of one of your favorite objects, such as fruit, bottles, vases, mugs, rocks, shells, a ball, books, or an interesting houseplant. Things that interest you most are always the best subjects. Smaller objects might be more suitable placed on top of the boxes. Overlap some of the items, and consider spotlighting one of your favorites by placing it farther away from the main grouping. Take a few minutes to really study where the objects are in relation to one another.

Study the objects

Let's Go!

Fig. 1: Lightly draw in the contours of the objects.

1. Start by deciding where the objects will be placed on the paper. Think about the size of your paper and the parts of the still life you want to show.
2. Choose your oil pastel colors and lightly draw the contours of the objects (fig. 1).

Fig. 2: Make short or long lines to fill in.

3. Fill in the objects with short or long lines, depending on whether the objects are smooth or textured or whether you want to follow a particular style (for example, an Impressionist painting) or work in your own style (fig. 2).
4. Use the side of the oil pastel to make broad strokes (fig. 3).
5. Use your finger to blend colors, and try to cover all of the white paper with color, just like a painting.

Fig. 3: Make broad strokes using the side of the pastel.

Go Further

Try this exercise with just one of your favorite stuffed animals, making your artwork very large—just like artist Joe Blajda did. You can even take your composition off the edge of the paper.

Meet the Artist: Joe Blajda

Joe Blajda is an oil painter and painting instructor. He created a series of paintings about his family's childhood stuffed animals. These oil paintings depict his sibling's animals in a personal and humorous light. This painting is of the artist's own childhood teddy bear. What do you think the bear is thinking?

Joe's Bear by Joe Blajda

Painting

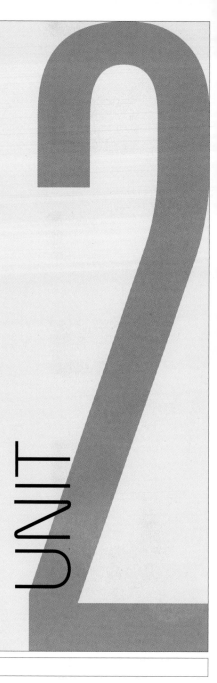

MOST PEOPLE HAVE HAD EXPERIENCE WITH PAINTING
from a young age, usually with tempera paint at a preschool easel, watercolor
at the kindergarten art table, or, for a lucky younger few, pudding on their high-
chair tray, with happy fingers swirling around! In the classroom, I rarely get an
objection from a student when we take out the paints for a session.

I believe the love of painting is something we all have as little children. I also
believe that nurturing that love through positive teaching methods can develop
a greater skill set within the medium, while retaining a satisfying creative process
at the same time. This Unit will guide us through a variety of water-based-media
painting experiences, whose end results will be a greater understanding of
color theory, value scale, visual texture, composition, techniques, and, most
important, an expansion of each person's own emerging style.

UNIT

- primed canvas or board
- pencil
- acrylic paints
- variety of small and large bristle brushes
- image of an artist's work
- water containers
- newspaper and paper towels
- Plexiglas palette

Think First: This Lab encourages you to paint through the eyes of a famous artist. Choose a master work that you are drawn to—and love. In this lesson, we are using Georgia O'Keeffe, but any artist you choose will do. Have a good copy of the original work, either from a book or the Internet, to work from.

Go further

- Try making the same work on a very large canvas, as Georgia O'Keeffe often did.
- When using another artist's work, try to use the same strokes; choose the same size brushes he or she used to actually "try on" the artist's style.

Let's Go!

Fig. 1: *Sketch the image on the canvas or board.*

Fig. 2: *Work from the back to the front of the painting.*

Fig. 4: *Add details.*

1. Begin by using a pencil to lightly sketch the contours of the image onto your canvas (fig. 1).
2. Mix the colors for the background and apply them in a thin layer, covering all the white primed canvas (fig. 2).
3. Working from the back to the front, add larger details, using smooth strokes and blending, just as Georgia did.

Fig. 3: *Blend the colors carefully.*

4. Mix some more paint and add a thicker layer of paint to the background, blending each color carefully. Continue to the front, adding final details as you go (fig. 3).
5. Pay attention to the subtle color changes, light to dark values, little details, and smooth color transitions that Georgia O'Keeffe used (fig. 4).
6. When you feel you are finished, add a protective coating, as described on page 11.

Meet the Artist: Georgia O'Keeffe

Georgia O'Keeffe was a beloved American artist. She lived in New York City when she was young and painted many of its buildings at night. Search online to see her well-known painting *The Radiator Building*. Visit www.okeeffemuseum.org to learn more about this artist.

Tiny Paintings on Wood

Materials

- small piece of smooth, gesso-primed wood
- pencil
- acrylic paints
- variety of small bristle brushes
- paper for sketching
- water containers
- newspaper
- paper towels
- idea for the subject of painting: small still life, landscape, abstract, or portrait
- Plexiglas palette

Think First: Making a small painting is a fairly quick exercise in getting an idea from your head into a painting. The paintings can be simple or detailed—the choice is up to you, the artist. Decide what you would like to paint from: a still life, photograph, abstract, or portrait. For our example, we used a sunflower as the subject matter. Going small can be a lot of fun. You can even make a tiny series of similar subjects, just like artist Daisy Adams does!

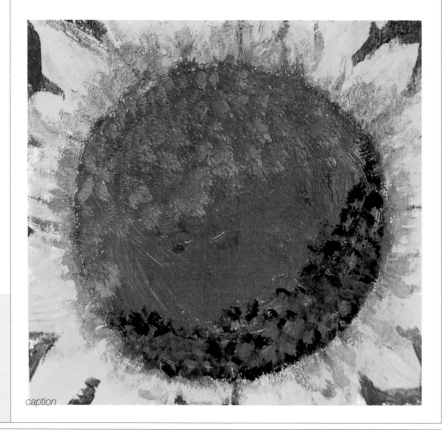

caption

Go Further

Make a series of paintings of the same object from different views or a portrait from the front and profile views!

Let's Go!

Fig. 1: *Paint in the background on the wood.*

Fig. 3: *Start the second layer.*

Fig. 4: *Use the right brush to make the right mark.*

Fig. 2: *Cover all of the surface.*

3. Add the second layer of paint, making sure that you are showing a good range of values (light to dark) and adding details that you feel are important (fig. 3).

4. Cut in the background, by painting in from the edge, if your subject is large and zoomed in, as in this example.

5. Use an assortment of small brushes, including flats and rounds, to make the strokes you want (fig. 4).

6. When you are finished, paint a protective coating over your artwork with a wide brush, or have an adult spray it with a clear coat as described on page 11.

1. On the gesso-primed piece of wood, begin by working the overall color for the first layer in the background. For our composition, we zoomed into the flower and started with yellow for the petals (fig. 1).

2. Working from the back to the front, add some larger details. Continue until all the surface is covered. Use the tiny brushes to make small strokes, or even dots of color, as you go for details (fig. 2).

Meet the Artist: Daisy Adams

Daisy Adams is an artist from New Hampshire. She owns a lovely shop called Lucy's Art Emporium, where she sells her work and the work of others in downtown Dover, New Hampshire. Her own work captures the kitschy, vintage feel of wayside America. Her work is often small in size and full of nostalgia.

Off To See the Wizard by Daisy Adams

Reverse Color Landscape Painting

- canvas, canvas board, or primed wood
- pencil
- acrylic paints
- variety of bristle brushes
- paper for sketching
- water containers
- newspaper
- paper towels
- photograph of an outdoor location
- Plexiglas palette

Think First: This Lab explores what happens when we use complementary colors for the base layer of our painting. This is an age-old technique that can really bring some instant depth to your painting. Find a photograph that really intrigues you and examine the light and color thoroughly. *National Geographic* magazines or photographs of places you have been are great for this.

Go Further

Try this method with an abstract subject, such as a scribble drawing! (See Lab 3.)

Let's Go!

Fig. 1: *Sketch the image on the canvas.*

Fig. 2: *Paint in the background.*

Fig. 3: *Use the right shaped brush for the shape area you are painting.*

Fig. 4: *Start the second layer with the actual color.*

1. Begin by drawing the horizon line on your canvas. Then include an outline of the most important features (fig. 1).

2. Set up your painting palette as described on page 11, the acrylic painting section.

3. Study the colors in the photograph, and then find a set of complementary colors in a color wheel. Use the primary color and its secondary complementary to begin your painting. Start by painting the background (figs. 2 and 3).

4. Work from back to front.

5. Refer to your color wheel to check your opposites! Mix in the complementary color to make the color you are painting with darker—don't use black.

6. When your base is dry, begin again

with the sky and paint in the actual colors (fig. 4). Leave some of the underpainting peeking through the edges for contrast.

7. Finish the top layer of paint with small details and let dry. Have an adult seal your painting when completely dry.

Meet the Artist: Christopher Volpe

"Also a poet, Volpe is drawn to the changing colors, lights, and moods of nature, like dusk and mist. It's the ability of his paintings to exude emotion and movement that distinguishes them from other New England landscapes, as well as a unique perspective and contemporary composition." —Chloe Johnson, journalist

Beginnings by Christopher Volpe

Watercolor and Salt Painting

Materials

list

- watercolor paper or cardstock
- set of pan watercolors
- soft-haired watercolor brushes
- small sponge
- newspaper and paper towels
- large water containers
- salt

Think First: The subject matter for this painting will come from your imagination. Because the effect of the salt on the watercolor is, in effect, a white or light speck, you might like to think of a subject that involves stars, sparks, tiny lights, snow, or rain. A dark background will render more contrast with the salt. A vibrant color will give a similar effect. Set up your watercolor painting area as described on page 11.

Go Further

Think of a subject matter for your painting in which the textural effect of salt would be useful: rocks, diamonds, caves, castles, sand, and fantasy creatures!

Let's Go!

Fig. 1: Begin painting with a very wet brush.

Fig. 2: Sprinkle the salt.

Fig. 3: See how the salt has moved the pigment.

1. Use your brush or a clean sponge to wet the paper. The brush should be wet, but not soggy!

2. Wet your brush again, and start to paint in your colors (fig. 1).

3. While the paint is still wet, but not in puddles, put some salt in one hand, and, using a pinching motion with your fingers, sprinkle it lightly in the areas where you want the effect. Deep, rich colors will produce a more vivid effect with the salt (fig. 2).

4. Remember, less is more—in the amount of salt and the amount of water.

5. When your painting is completely dry, rub the salt from the surface of the paper.

6. Admire the textural effect that salt has on your painting (fig. 3).

Meet the Author: Susan Schwake

"I have often used salt for texture in my watercolor work. This can be seen in the background of this collage illustration, *Evening Song*. I wanted to add interest to the watery lake and sky melting together, so I used salt to texture the two elements into one. I also had the lucky bonus of a rock shape appearing in the salt for the cricket to sit on."

Evening Song by Susan Schwake

Watercolor and Plastic Painting

Think First: Choose your favorite color combinations in your paint set. Think of how they might look together and how you would like to place them on your paper. Decide if you are going to mix new colors from the set for these artworks. Gather your supplies and set up a watercolor painting area as described on page 11. Cut plenty of plastic wrap to the size of the paper ahead of time—one piece sized for each piece of paper to be painted.

- heavy paper for watercolor
- plastic wrap
- watercolors
- soft brushes
- containers of water
- newspaper and paper towels
- scissors
- glue stick for gluing paper

Go Further

Use black ink to make a drawing over a painting you are not satisfied with. It's good to turn a piece of art you don't love into something else!

caption

Let's Go!

Fig. 1: *Start with a wet brush on wet paper.*

Fig. 2: *This wet-on-wet technique allows for spontaneous mixing!*

1. Use your brush to wet the paper. If your paper is large, wet it with a clean sponge.

2. Using a very wet brush and your predetermined color schemes, stroke the watercolor pans with your brush to load it with color.

3. Paint the color into the areas, filling the paper completely with as many or as few colors as you like (fig. 1).

4. Because the paper is wet and so is the paint, spreading will occur. This is called wet on wet and is a good thing! (fig. 2).

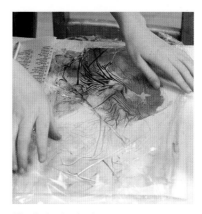

Fig. 3: *Apply plastic wrap.*

5. While the paper is still wet, place the plastic wrap over the painting with your hands and let it fully contact the paper. (fig. 3). Wrinkles are good. Encourage them by tickling the plastic wrap a bit (fig. 4).

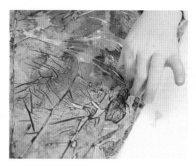

Fig. 4: *Encourage wrinkles by squeezing together areas of the plastic wrap.*

6. Do this to all of your papers. Let them all dry overnight. Don't peek!

7. Peel off the plastic in the morning and find your beautiful paintings waiting for you!

8. Keep the plastic wrap in a folder for the next time you want to make these paintings.

Meet the Author: Susan Schwake

"I often like to work with this watercolor method to create specific elements for my collages. I often tend to find insects, wings, ice, windows, and rocks in my paintings with this process. You can see this in my illustration entitled *Night Flight*."

Night Flight by Susan Schwake

Marker and Acrylic Painting

- canvas, canvas board, or primed wood
- pencil
- black permanent marker
- acrylic paint
- bristle brushes
- newspaper and paper towels
- water and containers
- Plexiglas palette
- mirror

Think First: This lesson encourages you to draw and to paint on the canvas, creating a modern, heavily outlined portrait. Using the mirror, examine your face and the shapes you can find in it. Your face will have one shape—your eyes, mouth, and nose other shapes. We will keep the contemporary graphic style of eliminating the background to focus on the portrait itself. Choose a background color before beginning.

Go Further

Try painting a group of your friends in this fashion. Work from a photo or ask them to pose for your pencil sketch!

Let's Go!

Fig. 1: *Use the black permanent marker over the pencil lines.*

Fig. 2: *Paint in the background.*

Fig. 3: *Paint a range of values of skin tone.*

Fig. 4: *Paint in the clothing.*

Meet the Artist: Darryl Joel Berger

Darryl Joel Berger is an artist and writer who works and lives in Ontario, Canada. Of his painting, Darryl says, "In many ways, this is really a drawing. I wanted to make something bold and graphic, something simplified and direct, like the best drawings can be. At the same time, I wanted to keep the kind of weight and thoughtfulness that you (should) find in paintings, so I applied the color in an abstract way, with plenty of power and movement." Find out more about Darryl at: http://red-handed.blogspot.com.

Pow Wow by Darryl Joel Berger

1. In pencil, make a light drawing of yourself on the canvas.
2. Go over the lines with the black permanent marker (fig. 1).
3. Set up your palette as described on page 11, for acrylic paint. Paint the background first with your solid color (fig. 2).

4. Mix your flesh tones to create a few shades of the color you wish to use for your skin tones. Paint these in next. Feel free to use the range of values found on your face (fig. 3).
5. Finish with your features and clothing (fig. 4). Go over any black lines that you painted over. Seal as described on page 11.

Materials

- watercolor paper, 90-lb. or more
- watercolor pans
- soft-haired watercolor brushes
- newspaper
- paper towels
- large containers of water

Think First: This lesson is experimental and process-oriented, allowing you to create an abstract, pattern-based painting. Start by selecting three to five favorite colors for your palette. Think of shapes you would like to include in this painting.

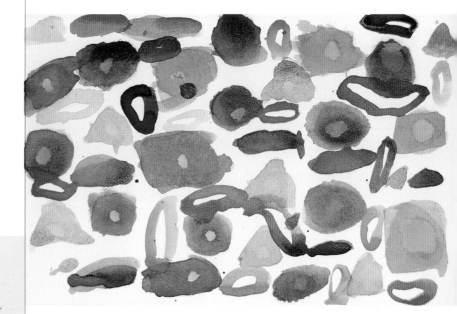

Go Further

- Paint large shapes that are filled in with one color. Let them dry completely, and then paint open-contour shapes over them.
- Make a painting with a limited palette of two colors.

Let's Go!

Fig. 1: *Start anywhere on your paper with your first color.*

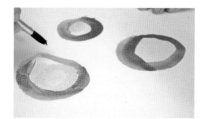

Fig. 2: *Repeat shapes in different sizes and colors.*

Fig. 3: *Try painting different shapes.*

Fig. 4: *Paint next to a dry area,*

Fig. 5: *Finish your painting.*

1. Load up a wet brush with your first color.

2. Starting anywhere on your paper, create areas of shapes and color (fig. 1).

3. Use a repeated shape in different sizes and colors to fill in areas. Use both light and dark values for the most impact (fig. 2).

4. Try painting different shapes together in the same colors, or paint the same shape in different sizes (fig. 3).

5. Let the watercolor paint dry before painting right next to it since wet areas that touch will run together (fig. 4).

6. Continue until the painting is as full as you wish (fig. 5)!

Meet the Artist:
Heather Smith Jones

Heather Smith Jones is an artist, arts instructor, and author from Lawrence, Kansas. Her work, entitled *Keep Going When You Are Not Sure,* is an inspiration for creating this lesson. It's important to always keep moving forward with your artwork. See more of Heather's beautiful work at heathersmithjones.com.

Keep Going When You Are Not Sure
by Heather Smith Jones

Printmaking

MAKING ART MULTIPLES IS AN ADDICTIVE PROCESS for most people. Printmaking is instant gratification at the most basic level, with the element of chance enhancing the technical process. The ability to create multiples of your artful idea—from a simple fingerprint to a sophisticated multi-plate foam print—is intriguing. This Unit explores many printmaking processes without the use of a press, from singular monotypes to multiple serigraph prints, to help students learn how to think in reverse, or in layers. A variety of papers and methods will produce endless variations on a theme from each Lab.

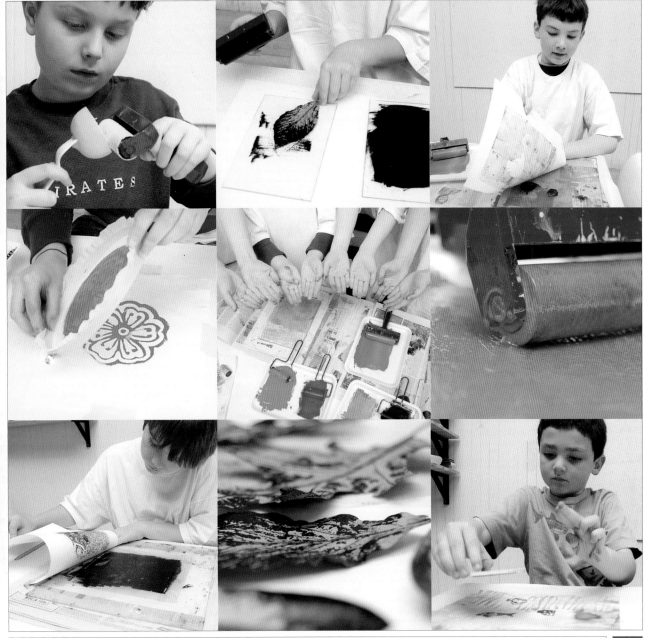

Found Objects Prints

- printmaking, sketch, or other smooth, medium-weight paper
- water-based printmaking ink in any color
- Plexiglas palette
- soft brayer(s)
- shallow dish of water
- paper towels
- newspaper
- white test paper
- objects to print, as described in Unit 1, page 9.

Think First: Study your objects and arrange them on your test paper. Do they make a face or a pattern? On the Plexiglas, roll out a small amount (a 1" [2.5 cm] circle) of any color of ink. Make sure it is somewhat smooth. Using the brayer, apply some ink to the object. Print the object onto the test paper to see the mark it makes. Experiment with the different objects you have chosen, and see what you can build with the marks you print. Try printing with only one "inking," to make lighter and lighter impressions, or use more or less pressure on the object when printing. Think about what a repeated pattern can do, too!

Meet the Artist: Terry Winters

Terry Winters is an American artist who works in printmaking, painting, and drawing. His *Folio* series inspired the circular prints in the Go Further section of this Lab. For more information on Terry Winters, visit www.moma.org.

Let's Go!

Test the print that each object makes first to plan your artwork.

Fig. 1: *Roll out the ink slowly and smoothly.*

Fig. 2: *Use the brayer to apply the ink to the object.*

Fig. 3: *Use firm, steady pressure to print your object.*

Go Further

- Try lace or other textured fabric on your print.

- Use the same object over and over to create a large area of one pattern.

- Your prints can go around and around a shaped piece of paper.

Prepare your area for printmaking as described on page 12. When you have decided on the subject or pattern you want to print, you are ready to begin.

1. On the Plexiglas, roll out the other colors you will use (fig. 1).

2. Using the brayer, apply ink in a smooth rolling motion to one side of the object. Dipping objects in the ink can result in too much ink, so try the brayer first. For a crisp, clear print of the object, less ink is better than too much ink (fig. 2).

3. Press the object onto the paper with a firm motion. Continue making your prints, using the brayer to apply the ink, until your piece is finished (fig. 3).

4. Let the print dry for several hours or overnight, either on a flat surface or hanging from a line with a clip.

Serigraphs/Silk Screen

Materials

- white or light-colored fabric
- wax paper
- sketch paper
- printing paper
- pencil
- nonwater-soluble glue (I like Mod Podge)
- acrylic paint
- acrylic textile medium
- newspaper
- paper towels
- Plexiglas palette
- sheer curtain or silk-screening material
- wooden embroidery hoop
- small bristle brush

Think First: Silk screening or serigraph is a stencil method of printmaking. You create a positive image by blocking out the negative space on the screen and pushing the ink through the remaining holes to create an easily repeatable print. You can use a simple design, with medium thick lines, and even text, if you desire. You can print on both paper and fabric, as we did. You can even make your own hand-printed shirts and scarves with this method.

Go Further

You can silk screen onto almost anything. Try making your own stationery, or put your own design on the edge of a tablecloth. Make a set of napkins to match.

Let's Go!

Fig. 1: Sketch out your idea first.

Fig. 2: Trace your idea onto the fabric carefully.

1. Draw your design inside a circle you have traced inside your embroidery hoop. Leave at least a 1" (2.5 cm) border all the way around the edge of your design (fig. 1).

2. Put your curtain or screening fabric in the hoop and tighten it well. Place it directly on the drawing and trace the design (fig. 2).

3. Using a piece of waxed paper underneath the hoop, apply the glue with a small brush. Block out the areas that you do not want to print. Check that all the holes are filled by holding it up to the light. Let the glue dry completely (fig. 3).

Fig. 3: Apply the glue with a small brush.

4. Mix two parts textile medium to one part acrylic paint. The mixture should be as thick as heavy cream. Lay your hoop on the surface to be printed. Using a bristle brush, paint the mixture with even strokes through your embroidery hoop stencil. Using a back-and-forth stroke gives you the most even print (fig. 4).

Fig. 4: Use a bristle brush to paint through the screen.

5. Lift the hoop when you are sure you have gone over all the areas thoroughly. Clean the screen well with the spray attachment on your sink, until the holes are all clear.

6. Let dry. Use a dry iron to set the print if you have printed on fabric.

Meet the Artist: Megan Bogonovich

Megan Bogonovich is a New Hampshire artist who introduced me to silk screening on clay. (But that is another lesson for another book.) Her work with silk screening on clay and her big ceramic sculptures have drawn international attention. She is a fearless artist, who I greatly admire. In the work shown here, she has silk screened her family photos directly onto the porcelain. See more of her fantastic work at www.meganbogonovich.com.

Family Jar with Lid by Megan Bogonovich

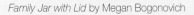

Fruit and Vegetable Prints

- assorted colors or white printing papers
- block printing ink
- forks for use as handles in the big fruits
- Plexiglas palette
- brayer
- newspaper
- an assortment of produce, such as lemons, mushrooms, peppers, apples, lettuce, and celery

Think First: Cut each fruit or vegetable so it has an even edge for printing. Lettuce is the exception to this rule. Onions make a great print, but they can make some people cry. Try them if you dare! Each piece of produce makes its own distinctive print. Consider combining shapes to make something representational, or make beautiful repeated patterns with the shapes. Using a fork as a handle in the larger fruits makes them easier to hold and print.

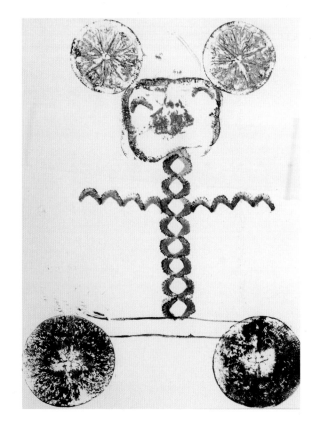

Go Further

These prints can make wonderful greeting cards or gift wrap.

Let's Go!

Fig. 1: *Roll the ink onto the produce.*

Fig. 2: *Press firmly!*

Fig. 3: *Repeat the printing process.*

1. Prepare your area for printmaking as described on page 12. Roll some ink onto Plexiglas.
2. Using the brayer, apply ink to the produce (fig. 1).

3. Make your print by pressing the produce firmly onto the paper (fig. 2).
4. Re-ink and keep going (fig. 3)!

5. Let the prints dry for several hours or overnight.

Meet the Artists: My Students

My students have made so many beautiful prints. I am featuring one of my favorites: a celery and mushroom forest. Colorful ink can be a fun change from black and white!

Colorful fruit and vegetable prints created by my students

Leaf Prints

- cardstock
- optional: wax paper
- pan watercolors
- black block-printing ink
- Plexiglas palette
- brayer
- newspaper
- paper towels
- assortment of leaves

Think First: Collect a selection of leaves in a variety of shapes. You can even try long-needled pine leaves and flat seed pods. Decide on some color themes for your background paper. You can use one color family, such as oranges, reds, and yellows, or paint a rainbow of colors!

Go further

You can print leaves onto a T-shirt by using the textile medium and acrylic paint as described in Lab 14. For washability, set the ink with an iron set on medium-high. Use a piece of paper inside the shirt and pass the iron over the print for three minutes.

Let's Go!

Fig. 1: *Paint the cardstock.*

Fig. 2: *Roll the ink onto the leaf.*

1. Paint your cardstock with your choice of colors and patterns (fig. 1).

2. Let the paper dry completely and prepare your ink as described on page 12.

3. With the back side of the leaf up, roll the ink-loaded brayer over the leaf, coating it fully (fig. 2).

4. Print the leaf by placing it on the paper (fig. 3). Rub it gently but firmly, to make a great print. You can use wax paper over the leaf to keep your hands free from ink.

5. Continue printing until you are satisfied with the final piece.

6. Let it dry for several hours or overnight.

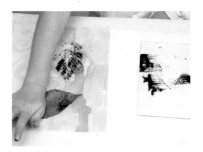

Fig. 3: *Print the leaf.*

Meet the Artist: Judith Heller Cassell

Judith Heller Cassell is a celebrated artist and member of the Boston Printmakers Association. This beautiful 3' x 4' (0.9 x 1.2 m) print hung in our gallery studio and inspired this lesson. Judith's prints are often in our studio gallery.

Persimmon Gold a monotype woodcut by Judith Heller Cassell

Cardboard Relief Print

- matboard or a strong piece of cardboard
- printing paper
- black block-printing ink
- Plexiglas palette
- brayer
- clear or white glue
- gesso and gesso brush
- an assortment of cardboard pieces

Think First: Sort through the cardboard pieces, and peel back some of the top layers to expose the corrugated part. Decide on a subject matter for your print—abstract is fun to begin with! You can sketch out a few ideas first of shapes you might use, if that helps your creative process.

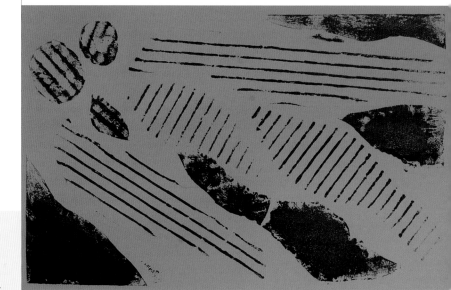

Go Further

These prints can be made with representational subjects, such as a landscape, a still life, or even a portrait. Just use the essence of the shapes for the best results.

Let's Go!

Fig. 1: *Expose the corrugated surface.*

Fig. 2: *Lay out and glue the pieces.*

1. Cut out your cardboard shapes. Peel away the top layer of some pieces to expose the corrugated surface; leave some pieces smooth (fig. 1).

2. Lay the pieces out on the matboard and glue them down. This will be your printing plate (fig. 2).

3. Let the glue dry completely, then gesso over the whole plate (fig. 3).

Fig. 3: *Paint the gesso on the printing plate.*

Fig. 4: *Roll out the ink on the plate.*

4. Prepare and apply the ink to the printing plate as described on page 12 (fig. 4).

5. Position the printing paper onto the plate and hold it with one hand, while rubbing over the paper in circular motions with the other hand. Peel off the paper to reveal your new print!

6. Continue with your prints to make an edition, as described on page 12.

7. Let them dry for several hours or overnight.

Meet the Artist: John Terry Downs

John Terry Downs was and is to this day my favorite art teacher. He was my professor for figure drawing and print-making and might be the best art teacher in the world. His prints, drawings, and paintings have been shown all over the world and have inspired hundreds of students. More about John can be found at www.plymouth.edu/department/art/faculty/profile/john-t-downs.

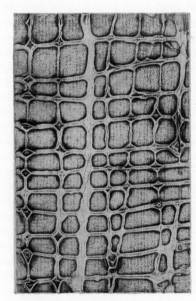

A collagraph print called *Pink Grid* by John Terry Downs

Paper

PAPER IS A STAPLE IN THE ART STUDIO, and most art budgets can include paper as a material for creating artwork. This Unit explores using paper as the medium for a substrate, as a structure, and for color, texture, and value. We will create collages, masks, and monsters from recycled maps, magazines, and other printed materials, as well as for your own textured papers. Paper can be used in art forms in endless ways. These Labs are springboards to other places, in which you can experiment with paper further and transform it with other media.

UNIT 4

Large-Scale Paper Fish

Materials

- 2 large sheets of white, heavyweight paper
- pencil
- watercolor pans
- soft-bristle brush
- scissors
- oil pastels
- newspaper
- paper towels
- heavy string

Think First: Your fish can be modeled on a real fish or made up from your imagination, just like we did in this Lab. Even the youngest artist can make a very big fish, with a little help from an older child. Examine some real fish in a tank or in a science book to figure out what shape to make your fish's scales. What color is your fish? What size fins and eyes will it have? Decide on the type of fish you want to make, and let's get started.

Go Further

You can make smaller versions of this fish and create a mobile, by hanging multiples from a branch you have found outside! Use tissue paper to stuff them.

Let's Go!

Fig. 1: *Draw in the details with oil pastels.*

Fig. 2: *Cut out the fish.*

Fig. 3: *Paint the fish.*

Fig. 4: *Staple around the edges of the fish.*

Fig. 5: *Stuff the fish with newspaper.*

1. Tape the two pieces of paper together. Draw the outline of the fish on the top piece with a pencil.

2. Add color with the oil pastels (fig. 1).

3. Using the scissors, cut the fish from the papers, being sure to cut through both pieces (fig. 2).

4. When the fish is free from the paper, open it flat to draw the other side.

5. Draw the other side of the fish with the oil pastels, as you did on the first side. Then, with the paper open flat, paint the whole fish with watercolor. The oil pastel will resist the watercolor and you will see your drawings perfectly (fig. 3).

6. When the fish is dry, staple it together, stapling most of the way around the edge of the fish, but leaving a gap. Get some help from an older friend, if you need it (fig. 4).

7. Wad up some newspaper into small balls and feed the fish until he is as fat as you wish him to be (fig. 5). Staple him shut, and hang him from a string!

Meet the Artist: Ulla Milbrath

Ulla Norup Milbrath taught high school art and ceramics and now teaches a variety of arts, including paper and fiber arts, jewelry design, and paper-clay sculpting in her studio in Northern California and at Castle in the Air studio in Berkeley, California.

Fabric Koi *by Ulla Milbrath*

Collage Tissue Self-Portraits

- paper
- pencil
- newspaper
- white glue
- water
- small container
- soft-bristle brush
- scissors
- tissue paper in assorted colors
- mirror

Think First: Did you know that you can mix colors with transparent tissue paper, just like paint? It's true! This lesson uses tissue paper, for the color and texture of the artwork, and glue, to hold the color in place. You can go with your natural colors or make yourself into a fantasy character, as our example shows.

Meet the Artist: Chuck Close

Chuck Close uses many different kinds of materials to make his portraits. In a portrait of his daughter, Georgia, he used more than thirty shades of gray paper to construct his 54" x 36" (137 x 99.5 cm) collage. His work is exhibited in many museums worldwide. To see it, visit a museum or check out the Internet.

Let's Go!

Fig. 1: *Draw yourself with a mirror.*

Fig. 2: *Glue the tissue.*

Fig. 3: *Glue and layer the tissue.*

1. Start by taking a look at yourself in the mirror. Study the shape of your face and begin drawing it on the paper. Add your features—your nose, eyes and mouth—but just in outline (fig. 1).

2. Mix one part white glue to four parts water. We will use this mixture to paint over the tissue paper, hold it, and seal it.

3. Using the scissors, or tearing the paper with your fingers, shape the pieces of tissue paper to fit your portrait. Using a brush, glue them down with the glue-and-water mixture (fig. 2).

4. Continue adding and gluing down the tissue paper, layering it where you wish the color to be darker and leaving a single layer in the areas you want lighter (fig. 3).

5. Add the background with additional tissue paper, using a solid color or pattern of your choice.

Go Further

This tissue paper method is great for other subject matter, as well. Try making a tissue paper still life filled with fruit and flowers or one of your favorite objects.

Torn-Paper Landscapes

Materials

- papers in assorted colors
- firm matboard for a backing
- glue stick
- scissors
- water dish
- paint brush

Think First: Landscapes can depict mountains, the desert, the beach, a lake, a forest, or almost anywhere on Earth! This lesson allows you to create a landscape out of your imagination. If you can't decide what to create, I recommend looking out your window or in a book for a reference. For our landscape, we imagined rolling hills on a sunny autumn day in New England.

Go Further

Make a series of landscapes of the same place in all the different seasons.

Let's Go!

Fig. 1: *For thick paper, use a paint brush and water to mark where you want to tear it.*

Fig. 2: *Tear thinner paper with your fingers guiding the way.*

1. Choose the colored papers for your landscape. We chose some hand-made papers in autumn colors.

2. To start the landscape, begin at the front of your paper, or the foreground, and work to the back, or the farthest away from you. If the paper is thick or hand-made, use a paint brush and water to mark where you want to tear it (fig. 1).

3. If your paper is not handmade or extra thick, you can just tear it slowly, with your fingers guiding the way (fig. 2).

Fig. 3: *Tear thick paper along the painted line of water.*

4. Continue tearing all the landscape papers to the sky (fig. 3). Create your landscape by laying out your papers on the mat board.

Fig. 4: *Glue the paper sky first.*

5. Beginning with the sky, glue your paper pieces onto the mat board with a glue stick, as described in Unit 1, page 25. Finish with the closest layer to the front (fig. 4).

Meet the Artist: Molly Bosley

Molly Bosley often works with cut paper as a medium. About her work, she says, "There is a tangible presence of hands in my artwork, meaning it is very obviously handled, touched, dirtied, and stepped on. It contains the imprint of the instrument that crafted it. The process is instinctive in choosing the images but structured, layered, and designed, so the different elements harmonize to produce an artwork that is wholly nostalgic." More about Molly's work can be found at www.mollybosley.com.

Tree House by Molly Bosley

Texture Monsters

Materials

- cardstock
- construction paper for background
- watercolor pans
- container of water
- paintbrush
- texture plates
- oil pastel
- pencil
- glue stick
- scissors
- newspaper and paper towels

Go Further

Monster cards are always a welcome sight for a birthday or a get well greeting!

Think First: Consider all the friendly monsters you have seen in books and in movies. Do they have horns or bushy hair? Perhaps they have big ears or long tails. You are the artist and you get to decide what features your monster will have. Because we will make the textured, colored papers ourselves and collage them together, you get to decide what colors your monster will be. You can sketch a few monsters out first, if you like—or not!

Let's Go!

Fig. 1: *Add texture designs to your paper.*

1. Choose a texture plate for your design and place your paper on top of it. Rub the oil pastel over the top of the paper to highlight the texture underneath (fig. 1).

Fig. 2: *Cut out the parts of the monster.*

2. Make several different texture patterns, so you will have enough papers for your entire monster. When finished, paint over the papers with a contrasting watercolor color. Let the papers dry completely.

Fig. 3: *Glue down the pieces.*

3. Draw on the backside of the paper with a pencil to create a guideline for cutting out your monster parts.

4. Cut out the parts and assemble them on the larger paper (fig. 2).

5. Glue down the parts, as described in Unit 1, page 25 (fig. 3).

Meet the Artist:
Rebecca Emberley

Rebecca Emberley has been writing and illustrating children's books for many years. "I like to do lots of other arty things," she says. "My current interest is silkscreening; I sew, I do graphic design work, and this year I even dabbled in music production. I have lived in many places and love to travel—it keeps my perspective fresh. I like to learn how other people live." Visit www. rebeccaemberley.com for more information on Rebecca and her talented family!

Beasties by Rebecca Emberley

Mixed Media

THE DARLING OF THE POPULAR ART WORLD for the past few years has been mixed media. It is no stranger to fine art, with Picasso and Braque leading the way, their first collage paintings hosting bits of lowly newsprint glued down amid the oil paint. The Labs in this Unit will inspire students to look for a second or third medium to complete a challenge in their work. Sometimes that means drawing with glue and adding color with magazine clippings. Other times the medium becomes the "drawn" line or subject matter itself. Mixed media is fun right from the start, and these Labs will produce different results each time they are used.

Make Your Own Collage Papers

- white cardstock
- watercolor pans
- soft paint brush
- container of water
- drinking straw
- shallow container for bubble printing
- liquid dish soap
- liquid acrylic paint
- old credit card
- newspaper and paper towels

Think First: This Lab is designed to create beautiful papers to use with other Labs. You can print on them, cut them up to use in collages, paint black ink on them, or make greeting cards, gift tags, and bookmarks from them. The possibilities are endless. Having a nice supply of hand-textured papers in the studio is always a good idea. The bonus of making your own is that you are doing just that: making. This Lab can really jump-start your creative process!

Go Further

Experiment with other methods of painting. We taped four paint brushes together and painted with them simultaneously!

Let's Go!

Fig. 1: *Tap with one finger.*

Fig. 2: *Blow beads of paint with a straw.*

Fig. 3: *Blow low in the container and slowly to avoid splurts!*

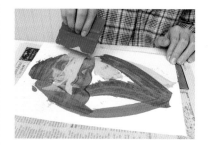

Fig. 4: *Acrylic smear painting*

1. Set up your painting area as described on page 11. We will begin with spatter painting. Load your brush with lots of water, then stroke the watercolor pan to get the color onto your brush.

2. Hold the brush over the paper and tap it with one finger from your other hand (fig. 1). This is called indoor spatter painting. No wrist or full arm fling required!

3. Now we will try straw painting. Load up your brush as in Step 1, but this time make small beads of watery paint all over the paper.

4. Place your straw very close to a bead and blow (fig. 2). Turn your paper to direct the movement of the bead. Remember to stop and take a few breaths in between bursts of air.

5. Bubble painting requires your straw again. In the shallow container, mix one part liquid paint to four parts water. Add half a part liquid dish soap. Blow low and slow through your straw into the container to make a bubble mountain (fig. 3).

6. Roll your paper over the top to print your bubbles!

7. Acrylic smear painting is fun and dramatic. Drip a few drops of liquid acrylic paint on the paper. Use an old credit card or similar tool to wipe the paint around the paper. Cover all of the paper with color (fig. 4).

Meet the Artist: Beth Olshansky

Beth Olshansky is the director of the Center for the Advancement of Art-Based Literacy at the University of New Hampshire. She is the developer of two art-based literacy models: Picturing Writing: Fostering Literacy through Art, and Image-Making Within the Writing Process.

A collage made with hand-painted papers by Beth Olshansky

Painting with Paper Inclusions

- canvas or board
- pencil
- acrylic paint
- acrylic medium
- paintbrush
- scissors
- palette
- newspaper
- assortment of papers
- easel

Think First: This painting relies on paint and paper to complement your subject matter. We chose to paint a small sculpture, made by the student. You can choose any subject. Examine your subject and decide which parts of the composition you would like to enhance with paper.

Go Further

Be inspired by a special ticket stub you find in your coat pocket, a letter you received in the mail, or even junk mail. Cut it up and create a mixed-media artwork based on the paper you are including!

Let's Go!

Fig. 1: *Sketch lightly on your canvas.*

Fig. 3: *Paint your canvas first.*

Fig. 4: *Glue the paper with acrylic medium.*

Fig. 2: *Cut and place the paper inclusions.*

variety of values in your color. Use an easel to work with the paint (fig. 3).

4. When the paint is dry, put your canvas flat on the table. Brush a little acrylic medium onto the back of your paper pieces and press them onto the canvas. Brush over the pieces with more medium to secure (fig. 4).

5. Continue with all the pieces, until finished. Coat the artwork with another layer of medium to seal it (fig. 5).

Fig. 5: *Coat the entire artwork to finish.*

1. Begin with a light sketch on your canvas (fig. 1).

2. Decide which parts of your artwork will have paper. Experiment with your composition by cutting those parts from the papers and placing them on the canvas (fig. 2).

3. When you are satisfied with the arrangement, set up the acrylic paint, as described on page 11 and paint your canvas, being mindful of the brush strokes you wish to have and the

Meet the Artist: Mati Rose McDonough

Mati Rose McDonough is an adult who paints like a child. It has taken her thirty-two years, two schools, and approximately 486 paintings to get to this point. Find out more about Mati Rose at www.matirose.com.

Red Elephant by Mati Rose McDonough

Acrylic and Ink Abstracts

Materials

- canvas board or stretched canvas (any size)
- India ink
- acrylic paint
- soft and bristle brushes
- Plexiglas palette
- palette knife
- drinking straw

Think First: Set up your workspace with a palette for acrylic paint, as described on page 11. Experiment with blowing one or two drops of ink across the paper with the straw. Keep the end of the straw close to, but not touching, the ink for best results. Turn the paper as you blow to direct the ink. Make sure to breathe normally between blows through the straw, or you might get dizzy!

Think about where you would like to place your first three dots of ink. Remember what happened when you did your test blows on the paper. Think beyond the first three, if you want to plan it out, or just go with the three and see what happens. Experimentation is a big part of art, and sometimes just going with the process is the best method. This exercise is part chance, part creativity, and all fun. It is all about finding images hidden in the ink splotches (or not!) then having fun pulling out all the stops with the paint.

Meet the Artist: Jen Garrido

Jen Garrido's artwork inspired this Lab and the negative-space drawing Lab (Lab 8). Of her work, Jen says, "I construct my paintings and drawings using a delicate balance of choice and process." You can see more of Jen's work at www.jenngarrido.com.

Windy but Holding by Jen Garrido

Let's Go!

Fig. 1: *Use slow breaths of air to control the ink flow. Short bursts of air will make the ink spray in all directions.*

1. Drop the first three ink droplets onto your canvas and blow them around until you are satisfied with the results (fig. 1).

2. Turn and examine the canvas to see if you have any emerging images. Make decisions about where to put more drops based on what you see (fig. 2).

3. Continue in groups of three drops at a time, until you are happy with the amount of ink and shapes you have on your canvas. Make sure some of your ink lines cross each other to make new shapes.

4. Let the ink dry completely while you dispense the acrylic paint on the palette, as described on page 11.

5. Looking at your ink blotches will tell you a lot about what colors to choose. You might end up with a face, a giraffe, a landscape, or a completely abstract design. Choose your colors to bring out the most important lines and shapes in your artwork (fig. 3).

Fig. 2: *Additional drops are added after looking carefully at the work, so far.*

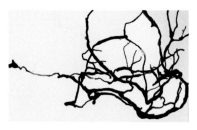

Fig. 3: *What do you see in your image? What colors are you going to choose to finish it?*

6. Follow the instructions in Unit 1 for working with acrylic paint. Use red, yellow, blue, and white to mix new colors on your palette with the palette knife (fig. 4).

7. Continue painting until you have filled in all the spaces between the ink blotches. Apply a second layer if

Fig. 4: *Use a palette knife to mix colors.*

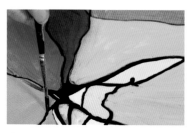

Fig. 5: *Repaint your black ink lines to make them stand out again.*

the paint seems too thin in places. Sometimes this happens with yellows and other light colors.

8. If any of the black lines have become painted over, go over them with the soft brush and ink. This will keep the lines of your images crisp (fig. 5).

Go Further

Try limiting your color choices to two colors, or use just one with the addition of white to make a range of values.

Watercolor and Pencil

- watercolor paper
- pencil
- watercolor pans
- paintbrush
- colored pencils
- container of water
- newspaper
- paper towels

Think First: Using a variety of media to create an artwork can be a ver natural process. In this Lab, we use a reference model (a book about birds) to create a imaginary animal based on features of a real one. Think about the parts of your artwork you would like to do in paint and which you would like to do in pencil. You can alternate between materials to get your desired results!

Go Further

Make a portrait, including a person or flowers, like our featured artist, Flossy-P, has!

Let's Go!

Fig. 1: *Paint color into the drawing.*

Fig. 2: *Draw with colored pencils.*

Fig. 3: *Draw in details.*

1. Find your reference material and begin your graphite pencil drawing on the paper.

2. Add color with the watercolor first (fig. 1). Remember that wet next to wet will run—which sometimes can be a good thing!

3. Continue with colored pencils for line definition or to add pattern (fig. 2).

4. Add small details with the pencils (fig. 3).

Meet the Artist: Flossy-P

Flossy-P lives in a small coastal village in Australia with her husband and new little baby boy. She says the ideas for her work come from seeing and becoming captured by things or moments or people that others usually wouldn't even notice. More of her delightful illustrations and artwork (and the story behind her name!) can be found at www.flossyparticles.com.

Curiosity by Flossy-P

Batik Landscapes

- washed and ironed white woven cotton fabric
- pencil
- liquid acrylics
- small containers for paint
- clear glue
- masking tape
- newspaper
- wax paper
- water containers
- dishpan
- Plexiglas

Think First: Batik is an ancient art form that uses wax to block out colored dye in patterns. The blocking process leaves a white line where the wax was. We are going to use clear glue for this process, instead of hot wax, and liquid acrylic paints, instead of dyes. Think about a simple landscape that you would like to make. Is there a lot of sky and a little land? What time of day or season is it? What is the weather like? Answering these questions will help you determine your composition.

Go Further

Use your batik fabric to make a cushion or a wall hanging.

Let's Go!

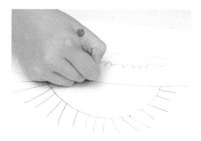

Fig. 1: Sketch your composition on paper.

Fig. 2: Apply the glue.

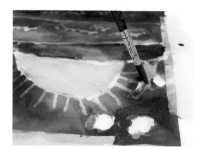

Fig. 3: Paint with liquid acrylic.

Fig. 4: Wash out the glue.

Meet the Artist: Batik by Nancy

Batik by Nancy is a little company from Brooklyn, New York. The owners, Tammy and Nancy, are a mother/daughter team who have created colorful batik clothing and accessories since the 1970s in their shop on Atlantic Avenue. Their work has been worn on television by the Cosby Show kids and by thousands of people all over the world. Each and every one of their pieces is made by hand. Visit them at 492 Atlantic Avenue, Brooklyn, New York, or online at www.nancybatik.com.

The Cow Jumped Over the Moon by Batik by Nancy

1. Sketch out your ideas first on paper with pencil (fig. 1).
2. Tape your fabric over wax paper attached to a firm backing, such as your Plexiglas plate.
3. Start drawing with the glue. Make sure you have a solid line of glue, so it blocks out the fabric from the paint. Let dry completely (fig. 2).
4. Paint the areas with the liquid acrylic paint. Don't scrub the brush too much over the glue. Let it dry overnight (fig. 3).
5. Wash out the glue with a little liquid soap and warm water. Scrub lightly with your fingers to get the glue out. Let dry and iron (fig. 4).

Resources

Australia
Eckersley's Arts, Crafts, and Imagination
www.eckersleys.com.au

Canada
Curry's Art Store
Ontario, Canada
www.Currys.com
art and craft supplies

DeSerres
www.deserres.ca

Michaels
www.michaels.com

Opus Framing & Art Supplies
www.opusframing.com

France
Graphigro
Paris, France
www.graphigro.com

Italy
Vertecchi
Rome, Italy
www.vertecchi.com

New Zealand
Littlejohns Art & Graphic Supplies Ltd.
Wellington, New Zealand
PH 04 385 2099
FAX 04 385 2090

United Kingdom
T N Lawrence & Son Ltd.
www.lawrence.co.uk

Creative Crafts
www.creativecrafts.co.uk

HobbyCraft Group Limited
www.hobbycraft.co.uk

United States
A. C. Moore
www.acmoore.com

Ampersand Art Supply
www.ampersandart.com

Dick Blick
www.dickblick.com

DecalPaper.com
www.decalpaper.com

Golden Artist Colors
www.goldenpaints.com

Hobby Lobby
www.hobbylobby.com

Homasote Board
www.homasote.com

Jo-Ann Fabric and Craft Stores
www.joann.com

Michaels
www.michaels.com

Preval Sprayer
www.preval.com

Pro Chemical and Dye
www.prochemicalanddye.com

Daniel Smith
www.danielsmith.com

Utrecht
www.utrechtart.com

The Art Lab Kids: Alicia, Alyson, Bella, Caanan, Chloe, Daria, Eilideh, Emily, Grace, Haiden, Ilona, Izabella, Jayden, Joseph, Kaleb, Kate, Keegan, Keith, Kelsey, Lauren, Liam, Maeve, Miles, Morgan, Robby, Robi, Skye, and Susan

About the Author

Susan Schwake is an artist, art educator, and curator. She actively exhibits her own work in galleries around the United States and Europe and sells her work online and in her own gallery, artstream. Susan has been part of juried public art exhibitions, creating large-scale, site-specific works.

Her passion for teaching and making art with others grew from a tiny seed of an idea in the fourth grade. Working in such diverse settings as schools, community centers, special needs nonprofits, summer camps, intergenerational facilities, libraries, and her own little art school, Susan has taught art to hundreds of people over the past twenty years.

She created a permanent exhibition of children's art, involving more than 100 local children, that graces the walls of a new children's room in her local library in 1997 and refreshed it in 2007 on the tenth anniversary. In 2000, she directed a similar project with 400 people in an intergenerational setting for a new multi-agency facility, bringing the staff, families, and clients more closely together through the process of making art. She has enjoyed many residencies in public and private schools, with whole school projects, and in special needs groups and single classrooms.

In 2005, Susan began a blog called artesprit. Through the blog, she embraced writing and photographing her world, meeting many new artists and friends around the globe.

She co-owns and is the curator for artstream in Rochester, New Hampshire. She enjoys bringing compelling group shows of contemporary art to New Hampshire. She is happy to be working alongside her husband every day doing what she loves most.

Blog: www.artesprit.blogspot.com

Website: www.susanschwake.com

Gallery: www.artstreamstudios.com

Acknowledgments

To everyone at Quarry Books who helped make this dream possible.

To Mary Ann Hall and Betsy Gammons for their guidance, patience, and encouragement. Thank you!

To my husband, Rainer Schwake, for his beautifully quiet way of helping and his endless support for me since the day we met. (I also am eternally grateful for his sweet photography skills.)

To my daughter, Chloe, who was tireless in her help with the lessons by making art spontaneously—and beautifully.

To my daughter, Grace, who nurtured the writing process.

To my intern, Bella, who was simply amazing.

To the parents of my students, for encouraging their journey in art.

To my students, who are deep inspiration for these lessons.

. . . and to all the kids who made art for this book—they rock!

Guiding Questions and Suggestions

In alignment with the core curriculum, these guiding questions and suggestions for teaching and learning can be adapted and applied to many of the activities in the labs, and support you, the teacher or parent, in incorporating these activities into the classroom or into the lives of your children.

1. Are you an artist? Certain attributes and attitudes are instinctive for artists-such as: focused attention to detail, a sense of wonder, a passionate curiosity, an active imagination, and a willingness to learn from mistakes. What other qualities do you think are important in great artists? Why? Which artistic qualities do you have?

2. What is mindfulness and why is it important to an artist? Are you mindful and observant of what is around you? For example, do you know what color eyes your family members or friends have?

3. Why is the process of making art so important to child development? In considering the cognitive domain of human development the author carefully guides young artists through lessons designed to learn and practice the art of higher-level creative thinking and critical analysis. Such terms as: *decide*, *predict*, *interpret*, *illustrate*, *create*, and *express* indicate the extraordinary opportunities for children to think for themselves as they become active participants in the learning process.

4. In considering the affective domain of human development, why is it important for a child to express his or her inner artist?

5. Susan Schwake believes, "through viewing the art of a wide variety of artists, students can identify with a particular movement or singular artist's work. This can reassure young artists of their own work, their own vision." (page 6) Which artist's work introduced in this book do your children prefer and why? Encourage them to seek out other works by the same artist and learn more about his or her style.

6. Let's talk about imagination. How imaginative are you? Do you picture things easily and clearly in your mind? Do you use your imagination to picture what you want to create before you begin drawing? If so, is it a vague idea or is it a complete image?

7. Appreciating nature's complexities, many artists gather inspiration from unlikely materials and resources, using a variety of media to create a work of art. Close your eyes and imagine a walk in the woods. What textures, colors, shapes, and sizes were combined to create the natural wonder all around you? Are you eager to explore and experiment with a second or third medium to complete your work? What results do you envision?

8. Within every lesson the author has presented opportunities for you to practice your measuring skills in real world mathematical situations. Think of all the things that need to be measured in planning and creating your work of art. Think of as many as you can.

9. Artists pay very close attention to their senses and often try to convey them in their work. Can you imagine all five senses in your favorite works of art? Can you express them in your own words? What are some ways to incorporate them into your art.

10. Colors can express moods and emotions. According to artist Pablo Picasso, "Colors, like features, follow the changes of the emotions." What do you think he means by that? Are there colors that make you feel happy, sad, strong, confident, peaceful, angry, fearful, or excited? What colors are they? Are there any colors that look gentle or soft?

11. Patterns are everywhere. A pattern is a design that is repeated over and over again. How many shape and color patterns can you can find in this room? What patterns do you see in the furniture or in the clothes people are wearing?

12. Each lab is plentiful with opportunities for enriching vocabulary with both general academic words and domain-specific words or phrases, as well as with relevant artistic terms. As you engage in lessons and activities make a list of unfamiliar words in the text. Look them up, create a glossary, and use them as you discuss your emerging artistic talents.

13. The author encourages both teacher-parent and child to "keep the fun part in mind when embarking on any of these labs—experience is the focus—not perfection." (page 14). While you may notice the child's achievements in complex cognitive, psychomotor, and affective skills, processes, and procedures through their work. It's important to release the child from your judgment of their art. It can be difficult to know when to provide what you consider to be helpful feedback and when to hold back. The most important thing to remember is that the child enjoys the process and is proud of what he has accomplished.

14. Susan Schwake believes, "The most important lessons in art are the ones that you discover about yourself in the process." (page 7) What are you discovering about yourself as an artist?

Adapted from guide written in 2015 by Judith Clifton, M.Ed, MS, educational and youth literary consultant.

Index